Gilbert & Sullivan for Singers

Soprano

Edited by Richard Walters

To access companion recorded accompaniments online, visit:
www.halleonard.com/mylibrary

1463-4291-0859-1389

Cover illustration: W.S. Gilbert created line drawings to accompany his librettos. His childhood nickname was Bab (derived from "baby"), and this was the name he signed to the drawings. They have become known as the "Bab Illustrations." From *The Mikado*, a demure Yum-Yum is shown contemplating a leering globe, illustrating her line, "Each a little bit afraid is, Wondering what the world can be!"

ISBN 978-0-634-05945-3

HAL•LEONARD® CORPORATION
7777 W. BLUEMOUND RD. P.O. BOX 13819 MILWAUKEE, WI 53213

Visit Hal Leonard Online at
www.halleonard.com

W.S. Gilbert

Arthur Sullivan

Contents

Because this role may be sung by either soprano or mezzo-soprano, the song is included in both volumes of the series.

The price of this publication includes access to companion recorded accompaniments online, for download or streaming, using the unique code found on the title page. Visit **www.halleonard.com/mylibrary** and enter the access code.

Plot Notes

THE GRAND DUKE
or *The Statutory Duel*

First produced at the Savoy Theatre, London, on March 7, 1896, with an initial run of 123 performances. The last Gilbert & Sullivan collaboration, it was not heard publicly again in London until a concert performance at the same theater in 1975.

A sharp tongued commentary on everything from Queen Victoria's German roots to Carte's preoccupation with money and Sullivan's Irish heritage, this operetta opens on a marketplace in Speisesaal, the capitol of the Grand Duchy of Pfennig-Halbpfennig in 1750. A theatrical troupe, with a manager named Ernest Dummkopf, is celebrating in advance of the nuptials of the leading comedian Ludwig to Julia. Julia muses on how she would behave as the Grand Duke's Bride, singing **"How Would I Play This Part."** The troupe members are part of a conspiracy to overthrow the Duke and put Dummkopf in his place. The Duke, meanwhile, is planning his own wedding to the exceptionally wealthy Baroness von Krankenfeldt. Convolutions of plot, including the infant betrothal of the Duke and misinterpretations of a secret, signal necessitate a duel. Traditional dueling is forbidden so a statutory duel takes place instead. The combatants draw cards, the higher card winning. The loser becomes "dead" for 24 hours. The winner is obliged to clear up all of the loser's debts and obligations before the "dead" person returns to life. Ernest and Ludwig duel, with Ludwig drawing an ace and winning. The Duke and Ludwig then duel with Ludwig drawing another ace and winning again. Ludwig quickly changes the law to keep the "dead" losers "dead." This, of course, creates romantic mayhem since the "dead" cannot marry, causing the sorrowful Julia to sing **"So Ends My Dream."** Just as the Prince of Monte Carlo arrives with his daughter to thoroughly muddy the waters, a notary points out that by law the ace is the lowest card. Since Ludwig won the duels with an ace, he is in fact the loser. The couples sort themselves back to rights and the curtain falls on the happy ending.

HMS PINAFORE
or *The Lass that Loved a Sailor*

First produced at the Opéra Comique, London, on May 25, 1878, with an initial run of 571 performances.

On the *Pinafore*, anchored off Portsmouth, the crew is proudly polishing and scrubbing the vessel as this satire on British class distinctions and military life opens. A woman named Little Buttercup comes aboard to sell them ribbons and lace for their sweethearts. Despite her merry demeanor, she carries a mysterious secret. Sailor Ralph Rackstraw, the smartest man in the fleet, declares his love for a young maiden. That maiden, unfortunately, is the Captain's daughter. The sailor Dick Deadeye appears with the unkindly explanation that Captains' daughters do not marry mere sailors. Enter the Captain. He explains to Little Buttercup that he is worried because his daughter, Josephine, has refused to marry Sir Joseph Porter, First Lord of the Admiralty. Josephine herself enters, singing **"Sorry Her Lot Who Loves Too Well,"** thus declaring her love for a sailor aboard the *Pinafore*, none other than Ralph. After her father explains the class issues involved with her romance she promises to forsake the sailor and reconsider Sir Joseph. Ralph finally summons the courage to confess his love to Josephine, only to have her respond coldly. A heartbroken Ralph threatens to shoot himself, but Josephine relents and confesses that she indeed loves him.

As Act II begins, the Captain paces the deck by night. He confesses his love for Little Buttercup but quickly explains that their different social positions make a relationship impossible. Little Buttercup cryptically advises him not to be too sure of that. Sir Joseph and Josephine enter. Sir Joseph is convinced that Josephine is intimidated by his high social standing; all the while she plots her elopement with Ralph, singing **"A Simple Sailor Lowly Born."** The evil Dick Deadeye informs the Captain of Josephine's upcoming elopement, allowing the Captain to stop the marriage. The crew steps in on Ralph's behalf, but the Captain curses at this behavior, which brings Sir Joseph out of the woodwork to berate him for speaking so rudely to a British sailor. Once Sir Joseph realizes his love intended to elope with Ralph, he orders the young sailor confined below decks. At the last moment Little Buttercup brings out the truth of her mysterious secret. Apparently she once worked as a nanny of sorts, and made a terrible mistake through which two babies were mixed up. Those babies were the

Captain and Ralph. So, in fact, the Captain is a mere sailor and Ralph is the Captain. Her news rings in a happy ending, as Ralph and Josephine, as well as the Captain and Little Buttercup, are freed from social restrictions and may marry.

THE MIKADO
or *The Town of Titipu*
First produced at the Savoy Theatre, London, on March 14, 1885, with an initial run of 672 performances.

The setting for this most popular of Savoy operettas is the courtyard of the Japanese Lord High Executioner in the town of Titipu. Handsome Nanki-Poo, a wandering minstrel, runs in looking for the lovely Yum-Yum. He has loved Yum-Yum for a long time and now that Ko-Ko, Yum-Yum's guardian and fiancée, is to be beheaded he sees his opportunity. However, Ko-Ko has been reprieved and enters to announce his new appointment as Lord High Executioner. As he discusses his wedding plans, Yum-Yum and two school-mates enter. Nanki-Poo apologizes to Ko-Ko for being in love Yum-Yum, receiving forgiveness. Later, Yum-Yum confesses to Nanki-Poo that she does not love Ko-Ko. Nanki-Poo confesses that he is actually son of the Mikado and is traveling in disguise to avoid marrying an elderly woman who mistook his good nature for affectionate advances. The Mikado meanwhile has sent word to Ko-Ko that if he doesn't execute someone soon his title will be abolished and the town reduced to a mere village. Ko-Ko spots Nanki-Poo about to end his life over his hopeless love, and asks if he might execute him since the lad is about do himself in anyway. Nanki-Poo agrees on the condition that he be allowed to marry Yum-Yum and live with her for one month before the execution. Ko-Ko agrees, being a more practical than romantic man. When Katisha, the elderly woman who wants to marry Nanki-Poo, arrives and tries to tell everyone of his true identity, she is ignored.

Act II opens on the preparations for Yum-Yum's wedding. Obsessed with her own beauty, she sings **"The Sun, Whose Rays Are All Ablaze."** But happiness dims when Ko-Ko learns that by law she, as the widow of Nanki-Poo, must be buried alive following his execution. A bribe to the Pooh-Bah (also known as the Lord High Everything Else) to fake a certificate of execution seems the best course of action until the Mikado arrives. When Katisha sees the execution certificate and tells the Mikado that his son has been executed, the Mikado promises punishment to all involved. Ko-Ko goes to Nanki-Poo for advice. Nanki-Poo advises him to marry Katisha. Ko-Ko woos her with the tale of a dicky-bird that died of a broken heart, and soon the two join in duet and then in marriage. Nanki-Poo, now free from Katisha's clutches, comes out of hiding and introduces the Mikado to his new daughter-in-law, thus ending the threat of punishment and the operetta.

PATIENCE
or *Bunthorne's Bride*
First produced at the Opéra Comique, London, on April 23, 1881, with an initial run of 578 performances.

A bevy of lovely maidens are gathered at Bunthorne's Castle as this satire on the aesthetic movement opens. All of the maidens are smitten with the poet Reginald Bunthorne, who has secret feelings for Patience, the village milkmaid. Only Lady Jane realizes the truth of his affections. Patience wonders why people in love never look quite healthy, singing **"I Cannot Tell What This Love May Be,"** so the maidens explain that they have always been in love. In fact they were once engaged to the Thirty-Fifth Dragoon Guards, who immediately march on stage followed by their Colonel. But they are no match, in the maidens' eyes, for poet Bunthorne. Bunthorne himself enters, seemingly engrossed in a poem he is composing but slyly listening to everything. As he reads his poem aloud the maidens become even more smitten with him. The Colonel reflects upon how he used to think a uniform would make a man irresistible. Bunthorne soliloquizes, explaining that he is an aesthetic fake. He then makes romantic overtures to Patience, who is not interested in love. But the maidens explain to Patience that love is a duty and she decides to fall in love. Another poet, Archibald Grosvenor, arrives and proposes to her. He reminds Patience that he is the boy she had loved as a child. Bunthorne, meanwhile, has decided to raffle himself off, only to be stopped at the last minute by Patience's offer to marry him. She indeed loves Grosvenor, but believes that she can only love unselfishly if she has no feelings for the object of her affections. The maidens decide to turn their affections back to the Dragoons, only to redirect them to Grosvenor the moment he appears.

As Act II begins, Lady Jane is deciding to forsake the Dragoons in favor of Bunthorne. She feels that they ought to marry in a hurry, explaining that she is not getting any younger. Grosvenor enters, with the smitten maidens traipsing along behind, making it clear that his heart remains with Patience. Patience now realizes that she should be with Grosvenor whom she loves, but duty requires that she keep her promise to marry Bunthorne. She sings a melancholy **"Love Is a Plaintive Song."** The rival poets are wildly jealous of each other by this point. Bunthorne demands that Grosvenor cease being an aesthetic and Grosvenor eventually agrees. Bunthorne decides to reform his unpleasant traits. Patience decides that loving the now perfect Bunthorne is hardly unselfish, so she feels free to love Grosvenor, who has become a commonplace, everyday man, as per his agreement with Bunthorne. Lady Jane and the maidens all marry Dragoons, leaving Bunthorne alone with his false poetry.

THE PIRATES OF PENZANCE
or *The Slave of Duty*
One performance, for copyright purposes, was given on December 30, 1879, at the Royal Bijou Theatre in Paighton, Devonshire. It opened officially for a run in New York at the Fifth Avenue Theatre on December 31, 1879. The London premiere was at the Opéra Comique on April 3, 1880, with an initial run of 363 performances.

Pirate festivities on the Cornwall coast open this satire on British military and constabulary, celebrating the completion of young Frederic's pirate internship. But Frederic is dejected. His situation is explained by Ruth, who had been his nursemaid. It seems that Ruth, being quite hard of hearing, mistook Frederic's father's instruction to apprentice him as a pilot and instead set him up as a pirate. The heartbroken Frederic must, for duty's sake, return to the honest world and work to end piracy even though this means betraying his pirate friends. He begs the pirates to give up their life of crime but they decline. Ruth begs Frederic to take her with him, as he has never seen another woman and considers the aging Ruth to be beautiful. Just then a party of beautiful young maidens appear for a picnic and are shocked to find a pirate in their midst. He pleads with them to take pity on him. Just when it appears that all will reject him, Mabel appears and bravely offers him her heart, with **"Poor Wandering One."** The other pirates spot the lovely maidens and creep in to kidnap them. The girls' father, the Major-General appears, hoping to foil the pirates' plans of marriage. He plays on his knowledge that Pirates of Penzance are orphans and are always tenderhearted toward other orphans, explaining that he too is an orphan and would be lost and lonely without his daughters. The pirates relent and the Major-General, Frederic and the girls depart, leaving poor Ruth with the pirates.

Act II opens in a ruined chapel, where the Major-General confesses to Frederic and Mabel that he is not actually an orphan. Frederic explains his plans to put the pirates out of business, and is in the process of proposing to Mabel when policemen arrive on their way to conquer the pirates themselves. They are just describing their grand plans when Ruth and the Pirate King arrive with a most ingenious paradox. Apparently Frederic was born on a leap-year day, so he won't actually reach his twenty-first birthday until 1940. Therefore he is still the pirates' apprentice. Always a slave to duty, Frederic returns to his pirate life, where honor forces him to tell the pirates that the Major-General is not an orphan. The policemen reappear and reluctantly prepare to arrest the pirates. The pirates meanwhile can be heard sneaking up on the Major-General. Just as the pirates are about to do in the Major-General, the policemen leap to his defense, only to be defeated almost immediately. They are about to be killed when the police pull Union Jacks from their pockets and command the pirates to stand down in the name of Queen Victoria. The pirates, who love their Queen, comply. Ruth puts everything to rights by explaining that the pirates are actually noblemen who have gone wrong. They are immediately forgiven and given back their titles. Frederic and Mabel reunite and the Major-General asks the pirates/nobles to marry his daughters.

PRINCESS IDA
or *Castle Adamant*
First produced at the Savoy Theatre, London, on January 5, 1884, with an initial run of 246 performances. *Princess Ida* is the only three-act operetta by Gilbert and Sullivan.

This satire on women's suffrage and Darwin's evolutionary theories opens on a scene of great expectation. Prince Hilarion awaits the arrival of Princess Ida, to whom he has been betrothed since infancy. But her father, King Gama, arrives without her, explaining to the Prince and his father King

Hildebrand that Princess Ida is now running a school for girls at Castle Adamant. There they study the classics and the villainy of men. Hildebrand and Hilarion decide to hold Gama and his three sons as hostages while they storm the Castle Adamant to claim the Princess.

At the Castle Adamant, the Princess sings **"Oh, Goddess Wise"** in reverie of Minerva, the Goddess of Wisdom. Lady Psyche, Professor of Humanities, instructs her students that man is ape at heart, in **"A Lady Fair of Lineage High."** Hilarion and two friends scale the castle wall and disguise themselves in women's clothing. With several of the women aware of the men, and keeping their secret, the three pull off the ruse for a time. But after drinking a bit too much, one of the men gives up the secret. Princess Ida orders the men's arrest. But King Hildebrand has massed his troops outside the castle walls to force Ida to make good on the betrothal. He gives her twenty-four hours to make up her mind, threatening to raze the castle and hang her brothers and father if she declines.

The Princess decides to fight, but her students are in terror of hurting someone so they refuse. When her father returns, crestfallen after such obsequious treatment at the Hildebrand palace, Ida's resolve weakens and she sings **"I Built Upon a Rock."** Meanwhile King Hildebrand has decided that fighting women is in poor form, so he has Ida's brothers brought from his castle to fight for the women against Prince Hilarion and his two friends. Hilarion and company win. Princess Ida marries Hilarion, and two of her colleagues marry his friends. Lady Blanche is left to fulfill her dream of running the school and the curtain falls.

RUDDIGORE
or *The Witch's Curse*
First produced at the Savoy Theatre, London, on March 14, 1885, with an initial run of 288 performances.

The professional bridesmaids in the Cornish village of Rederring are antsy for work. The lovely Rose Maybud is the most likely candidate, but she keeps rejecting suitors. She sings **"If Somebody There Chanced to Be,"** explaining that she is waiting for the right person. Rose's Aunt Hannah tells of Sir Roderic Murgatroyd of Ruddigore, her lost love. Roderic defied the curse of the Murgatroyd heirs, which condemns them to commit a crime each day or perish, and died on their wedding day. Despard Murgatroyd has assumed the title and is living the obligatory life of crime. The shy Robin Oakapple, who is really Sir Ruthven Murgatroyd, appears. Robin explains that he is too shy to approach Rose. Robin's half brother, a sailor named Richard, offers to woo Rose on Robin's behalf, but falls madly in love with her and woos her for himself instead. When Robin learns of this betrayal he poisons Rose's mind against sailors and she turns her affections to him. At this point Mad Margaret enters. Driven to insanity by her passion for Despard, she is wildly jealous of Rose, who reassures her. The plot thickens when Robin reveals himself as Despard's older brother, whom all thought was dead. Robin's title is restored and Rose leaves him for Despard. But Despard spurns her, going back to Margaret. Rose returns to Richard and Robin collapses.

Act II opens with a haggard Sir Ruthven (Robin) in the picture gallery of his castle, looking for a crime to commit. Rose and Richard have come to ask permission to marry and Ruthven threatens to imprison Rose as his crime of the day. Richard pulls out a Union Jack, which of course even the worst of criminals cannot ignore, and the two leave safely. At this point the portraits of the previously cursed Murgatroyds come to life to remind Ruthven what will happen if he fails to commit a crime. Ruthven wearily sends someone off to kidnap a maiden on his behalf, which brings Hannah to the castle. In the meantime Despard and Margaret, now school masters, arrive to encourage Ruthven to reform. They add that under the law Ruthven is responsible for Despard's crime as well as his own. Ruthven vows to reform, no matter what the consequences. With Hannah in the room, Ruthven calls upon the picture of his Uncle Roderic to help him. Roderic's picture comes to life and he spots Hannah. Ruthven leaves, contemplating his predicament. But the day is saved when Ruthven rushes back in with a brainstorm. Failing to commit a crime each day while knowing the sentence for such action is death, he reasons, is tantamount to suicide. Since suicide is a crime in and of itself, Sir Roderic should never have died. This means that all concerned may pair off as they see fit and thus ends the curse and the operetta.

THE SORCERER
First produced at the Opéra Comique, London, on November 17, 1877, with an initial run of 178 performances.

The village of Ploverleigh is percolating with affection as this satire on Victorian society opens. Aline Sangazure glories in her engagement to Alexis Poindextre of the Grenadier Guards. Villager Constance Partlet harbors secret feelings for Dr. Daly, the Vicar, which she reveals in **"When He Is Here."** Daly is oblivious of Constance's feelings. Constance's mother, meanwhile, has her eye on the Notary. Aline sings **"Happy Young Heart,"** rapturously anticipating her impending nuptials. Aline and Alexis, hoping to share their loving bliss with the entire village, hire a sorcerer to drug the community with a love-at-first-sight potion. The potion is administered through tea at a village picnic. Everyone but the young lovers and the sorcerer drinks the potion-spiked tea and falls into a deep sleep.

As midnight strikes the villagers begin to awaken, immediately falling head-over-heels in love with the first person they happen to spot. Seeing the potion's effects, Alexis asks Aline to drink the potion, to deepen their love for each other. She refuses, causing a quarrel. Eventually she agrees, but spots Dr. Daly immediately afterward and falls in love with him instead of her betrothed Alexis. The potion-induced romances have made a mess of things. Alexis' father, Sir Marmaduke has fallen for Mrs. Partlet, while Lady Sangazure has become smitten with Mr. Wells and Constance with the Notary. It becomes apparent that either Alexis or Mr. Wells must give his life to the forces of evil to break the spell. Neither is willing so a vote is taken. The sorcerer loses and is swallowed up by the earth as a gong sounds. The potion's spell is broken and the villagers return to their original affections.

THE YEOMEN OF THE GUARD
or *The Merryman and His Maid*
First produced at the Savoy Theatre, London, on October 3, 1888, with an initial run of 423 performances.

The year is fifteen-hundred-and-something. Young Phoebe Meryll ponders the heartbreaks of love. She is pining for the dashing Colonel Fairfax who sits in the Tower of London awaiting execution for the crime of sorcery. He was accused of the crime by his scheming cousin. Should he die without a wife, Fairfax explains to the Lieutenant, his title and wealth transfer to the cousin. He begs the Lieutenant to marry him to the poorest woman that can be found so that she might inherit his name and wealth instead. Meanwhile Wilfred, Head Jailor and Assistant Tormentor of the Tower of London, has eyes for Phoebe. While she once thought him fine, she has since become enamored of the Colonel and will have nothing to with Wilfred. Jester Jack Point and singer Elsie Maynard enter. A less than appreciative crowd threatens to mob them but the Lieutenant saves them, immediately marrying Elsie to Fairfax. Elsie returns from the hasty ceremony and sings **"Tis Done! I Am a Bride."** Meanwhile, Phoebe has come up with a plan. She flirts with Wilfrid and steals his keys just long enough for her father to free Fairfax. Wilfrid is barely gone when Fairfax appears in the uniform of the Yeomen of the Guard, posing as the son of Sergeant Meryll. As Phoebe and her "brother" give each other an uncommonly affectionate greeting, the bells toll the hour of the execution. Guards rush back with the news that Fairfax has escaped.

Act II finds Jack Point feeling regret for allowing Elsie to marry Fairfax. It seemed a better idea when Fairfax was about to die, since Jack wanted to marry Elsie himself and figured Fairfax's money would be welcome. He advises Wilfrid on the hazards of jesting. The newly freed Fairfax is putting the fidelity of his new wife to the test, masquerading as Leonard Meryll. Jack and Wilfrid conspire to fake Fairfax's death, saying that they shot the Colonel as he dove into the river. With Fairfax thought dead, Jack proposes to Elsie, who rejects him. Fairfax wonders who his new bride might be, only to discover moments later that his bride is Elsie. Phoebe, distraught over loosing Fairfax tells Wilfrid of the escape and disguise. Wilfrid forces her to marry him to keep the secret. Suddenly the real Leonard appears with an official pardon for Fairfax. Elsie, at first heartbroken to learn that her real husband is alive is delighted when it is revealed that her beloved Leonard is really Fairfax and therefore they are married. Jack, the only one left without a spouse, falls to the ground in a faint.

Gilbert & Sullivan for Singers

Soprano

How Would I Play This Part

THE GRAND DUKE

Words by W.S. Gilbert
Music by Arthur Sullivan

Allegretto grazioso

JULIA:

How would I play this ___ part— The Grand Duke's Bride? All

ran - cour ___ in my ___ heart I'd du - ly hide—

I'd drive it from ___ my ___ re - col - lec - tion And 'whelm him with ___ a ___

12

So Ends My Dream

THE GRAND DUKE

Words by W.S. Gilbert
Music by Arthur Sullivan

So ends my dream— so fades my vi-sion fair! Of

hope no gleam— dis-trac-tion and des-pair! My cher-ish'd dreams, the

Du-cal throne to share, That aim su-preme has fad-ed in-to

Andante con molto espressione

air! ___ All _ is dark - some— All _ is drea - ry— Bro - ken ev - 'ry pro - mise plight - ed— Sad _ and sor - ry— weak _ and wea - ry, Ev - 'ry new - born hope _ is blight - ed! Death _ the Friend or Death _ the Foe, Shall _ I

call up - on ___ thee? No!   I __ will go on liv - ing,

liv - ing,   tho' Sad _ and sor - ry—__ weak _ and wea - ry!   Death _ the

Friend or Death _ the Foe,   Shall _ I call up - on ___ thee?

No!   I _ will go on liv - ing, liv - ing,   Sad _ and

cresc.

20

Ah!

f Gaily

No, no! Let the by - gone go by! For no good ev - er
came of re - pin - ing: If to - day there are clouds o'er the
sky, Yet to - mor - row the sun may be shin - ing! To -

p

[simile]

22

23

24

The Sun, Whose Rays Are All Ablaze
THE MIKADO

Words by W.S. Gilbert
Music by Arthur Sullivan

YUM-YUM:

1. The sun, whose rays Are all a - blaze With ev - er - liv - ing glo - ry,
2. Ob - serve his flame, That plac - id dame, The moons Ce - les - tial High - ness;

Does not de - ny His maj - es - ty— He scorns to tell a sto - ry!
There's not a trace Up - on her face Of dif - fi - dence or shy - ness:

He won't ex-claim, "I blush for shame, So kind-ly be in-dul - gent;"
She bor-rows light That, thro' the night, Man-kind may all ac-claim her!

But, fierce and bold, In fier-y gold, He glo-ries all ef-ful - gent.
And, truth to tell, She lights up well, So I, for one, don't blame her.

I mean to rule the earth, _____
Ah, pray make no mis - take, _____

A Simple Sailor Lowly Born

HMS PINAFORE

Words by W.S. Gilbert
Music by Arthur Sullivan

Where organs yell, and clacking housewives fume, And clothes are hanging out all day a - dry-ing, With one cracked looking-glass to see your face in, And

Allegro con spirito

dinner served up in a pudding - bas - in!

cresc. molto

A sim - ple sail - or, low - ly born, Un -

let - tered and un - known, Who toils for bread from ear - ly morn Till

half the night has flown, Till half the night has flown! No

gold - en rank can he im-part, No wealth of house or land, No

cresc.
for - tune, save his trust - y heart, And hon - est, brown right hand, his trust - y

heart, and brown right hand! And yet he is so won - d'rous fair, That

love for one so pass - ing rare, So peer - less in his man - ly beau - ty, Were

lit - tle else than sol - emn du - ty, Were lit - tle else than sol - emn

rall. *ad lib.*

du - ty! Oh, god of love, and god of rea - son, say, ___ Which of you

a tempo

twain shall my poor heart o - bey! A sim - ple sail - or, low - ly born, Un -

let - tered and un - known. _____ No gold - en rank can he im-part, No

wealth of house or land, No for - tune, save his trust - y heart, And

hon - est, brown right hand, his trust - y heart and right hand! Oh, god of

cresc.

love, and god of rea - son, say, Which of you twain shall

god of love, and god of rea - son, say, Which of you twain shall my poor

heart _____ o - bey, ____ my ____ heart ____ o -

bey, Which shall my heart, _____ my heart o -

bey!

bey!

Sorry Her Lot Who Loves Too Well

HMS PINAFORE

Words by W.S. Gilbert
Music by Arthur Sullivan

I Cannot Tell What This Love May Be

PATIENCE

Words by W.S. Gilbert
Music by Arthur Sullivan

Love Is a Plaintive Song

PATIENCE

Words by W.S. Gilbert
Music by Arthur Sullivan

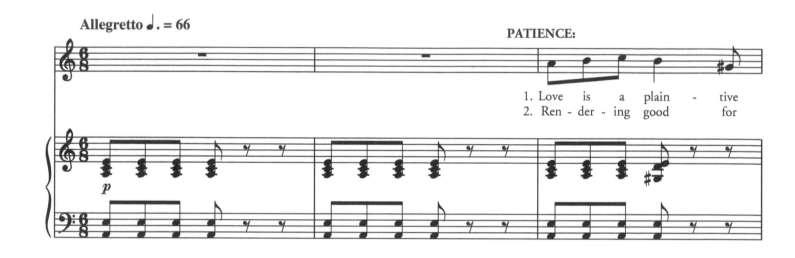

trayed; Tuned to each chang - ing note, Sor - ry when *he* is
down, Nev - er a self - ish whim, Trou - ble, or pain to

sad, _____ Blind to his ev - 'ry mote, Mer - ry when he ___ is
stir; _____ Ev - e - ry - thing for him, Noth - ing at all ___ for

rall. *a tempo*

glad! Mer - ry when he ___ is glad! _____ Love that no
her! Noth - ing at all ___ for her! _____ Love that will

rall. *a tempo* *p*

wrong can cure, Love that is al - ways new, That is the love that's
aye en - dure, Though the re - wards be few, That is the love that's

pure, _____ That is the love _ that's true! _____ Love that no
pure, _____ That is the love _ that's true! _____ Love that will

cresc.

wrong can cure, Love that is al - ways new,
aye en - dure, Though the re - wards be few,
} That is the love _ that's

f

pure, That _____ is _____ the love, _____ the love _____ that's

ad lib.

colla voce

a tempo

true! _____

f a tempo

Poor Wand'ring One
THE PIRATES OF PENZANCE

Words by W.S. Gilbert
Music by Arthur Sullivan

mine! Ah! _____ Ah! _____ Ah! ___

cres -

_____ Ah, _____

cen - do *f*

Poor wan - d'ring one! _____ Though thou hast sure - ly

strayed, _ Take heart of grace, Thy steps re - trace,

Ah! ah! _____

Ah, _____ Take heart!

I Built Upon a Rock

PRINCESS IDA

Words by W.S. Gilbert
Music by Arthur Sullivan

leant up - on an oak, But in the hour of need, A - lack - a - day, My trust - ed stay Was

cresc.

but a bruis - ed reed! a bruis - ed reed!

Ah, faith - less rock, My sim - ple faith to mock!

Ah, trai - t'rous oak, Thy worth - less - ness to cloke, Thy worth - less - ness to

cloke!

2. I

drew a sword of steel, But when to home and

way, had died a - way! Ah, cow - ard

steel That fear can un - an - neal!

sempre f

False fire in - deed, To fail me in my need, To fail me in my

need!

Oh, Goddess Wise
PRINCESS IDA

Words by W.S. Gilbert
Music by Arthur Sullivan

I may lead them to thy sa - cred shrine!

Let fer - vent words and fer - vent thoughts be mine, That I _____

_____ may lead them to thy sa - cred _____ shrine _____ I _____ may _____ lead them to thy

sa - cred shrine, thy sa - cred shrine!

cresc. molto

ff

A Lady Fair of Lineage High

PRINCESS IDA

Words by W.S. Gilbert
Music by Arthur Sullivan

would not do— His scheme fell through, For the

Maid, when his love took for - mal shape, Ex - press'd much ter - ror At his mon - strous er - ror, That he

stam - mer'd an a - po - lo - gy and made his 'scape, The pic - ture of a dis - con - cert - ed Ape.

2. With a

64

65

Maid was Beau-ty's fair-est Queen, With gold-en tress-es, Like a real prin-cess-'s, While the

Ape, de-spite his___ ra-zor keen, Was the A-pi-est Ape that ev-er was seen!

ff

pesante

3. He bought white ties, and he

p

bought dress suits, He cramm'd his feet in-to bright tight boots——— And to

66

If Somebody There Chanced to Be

RUDDIGORE

Words by W.S. Gilbert
Music by Arthur Sullivan

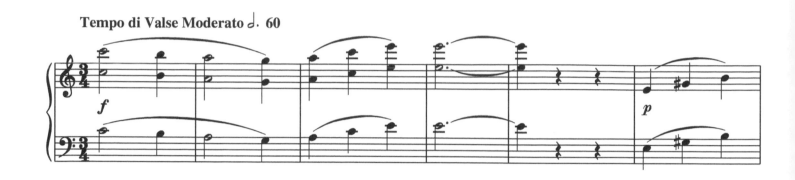

Tempo di Valse Moderato ♩. 60

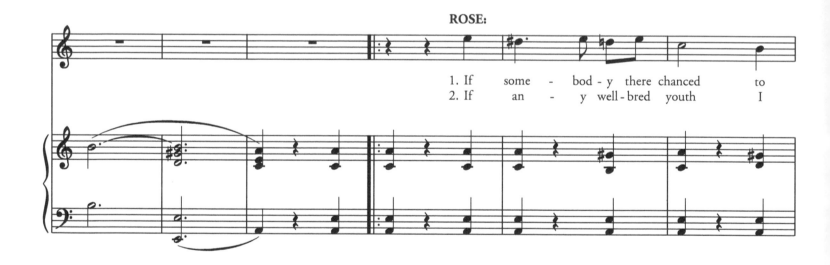

ROSE:

1. If some - bod - y there chanced to
2. If an - y well - bred youth I

be
knew,

Who loved me in a man - ner true,
Po - lite and gen - tle, neat and trim,

My
Then

70

Ah! _____ Had I the love of such ___ as
Ah! _____ And if I loved of him through _ and

he, Some qui - et spot he'd take ___ me to, Then he could
through— (True love and not a pass - ing whim), Then I could

whis - per it to me, _____ And I could whis - per it to
speak of it to you, _____ And you could speak of it to

you. _____ But whis - per - ing, I've some - where
him. _____ But here I find it does - n't

(referring to book)

When He Is Here

THE SORCERER

Words by W.S. Gilbert
Music by Arthur Sullivan

hope, no hope, no so - lace, no al - loy!

2. When I re - joice, He shows no

plea - sure, When I am sad, It grieves him not. His

76

Happy Young Heart
THE SORCERER

Words by W.S. Gilbert
Music by Arthur Sullivan

My kind - ly friends, I thank you for this greet - ing. And so you wish me ev - 'ry earth - ly joy,

I trust your wish - es may have quick ful - fil - ment!

Oh, hap - py young heart! _____ Comes thy young lord a -
Oh, mer - ry young heart! _____ Bright are the days of

'Tis Done! I Am a Bride
THE YEOMEN OF THE GUARD

Words by W.S. Gilbert
Music by Arthur Sullivan

sad - ness? A bride-groom all un - known, save in

Allegro, un poco agitato ♩. = 84

this wise, To - day he dies! To - day, a - las, he dies!

1. Though tear and long - drawn sigh
2. Ere half an hour has rung, A

Ill fit a bride, No sad - der
wid - ow I! Ah, heav'n, he